I0171513

Ten Marbles and a Bag to Put Them In
Poems for Children

By DuEwa Frazier

Published by
Lit Noire Publishing
P.O. Box 26183
Brooklyn, New York 11202-6183
EMAIL duewa_frazier@litnoirepublishing.com

1st Edition Paperback
Copyright © 2010 DuEwa Frazier, Lit Noire Publishing

Manufactured in the United States of America
Layout: DuEwa Frazier

No part of this publication may be reproduced, stored in a retrieval system, or transmitted in any form or by any means, electronic, mechanical, photocopying, recording, scanning, or otherwise accept by written permission of the publisher.

Ten Marbles and a Bag to Put Them In/DuEwa Frazier

ISBN-10: 0-9719052-4-X
ISBN-13: 9780971905245

   I.   Frazier, DuEwa

Printed in the United States of America

10 9 8 7 6 5 4 3 2 1

Ten Marbles and a Bag to Put Them In
Poems for Children

By DuEwa Frazier

Lit Noire Publishing

New York

Other books by DuEwa Frazier

Check the Rhyme: An Anthology of Female Poets & Emcees (2006, Lit Noire Publishing)

Stardust Tracks on a Road (2005, Lit Noire Publishing)

Shedding Light From My Journeys (2002, Lit Noire Publishing)

For Tamara and Janelle Springfield of St. Louis, MO
And for the children at The Wyman Center in St. Louis

Acknowledgements & Thank You

This collection has been in progress for many years. *Ten Marbles* is for elementary school children, and their parents and teachers.

Since moving to New York, I have enjoyed working for schools and non-profit organizations. I have taught both English and Theater Arts for secondary students in New York City. I have also shared my poetry and taught workshops for the "It's All About Me" rites of passage program sponsored by New York City Mission Society. I have had quite an amazing journey as an educator, writer, and advocate for youth literacy.

I wish to thank my parents, Sylvia J. Wilson Frazier and Eric Frazier for their continued support. Thank you to the following children's authors, schools and, organizations: The New School MFA Writing for Children program, Morningside Alliance-Read Out Loud, Christine Petro, Jerry Craft, Lindamichellebaron, Javaka Steptoe, Tonya Hegamin, Rocket Learning, Kwame Alexander, Willie Perdomo,

Hue Man Bookstore, New York City Mission Society, New York City

Public Schools, AALBC, Mosaic Books, and The Harlem Book Fair.

Many thanks to all of the young readers!

DuEwa Frazier

Brooklyn, NY

June 2010

Poems

Mommies

Mommies are fun

sweet and cuddly

Mommies will wipe

your tears

and sing

your blues

away

Mommies will kiss you

in the morning before school,

and say, "Have a good day!"

Mommies work hard in and

outside of the house

Mommies make the best

cookies, pies and cakes

Mommies know when you

have a tummy ache

Mommies were once little

children too

maybe that's why they know

how to take such good

care of you

Mommies are tall, short,

skinny or round

Mommies are good to us

every minute

all year round

"Mommies" Questions:

1. What kinds of fun things do you do with your mommy?

2. What is something you would like to do with your mommy?

Activity

Draw a picture of your mommy wearing her favorite outfit. Does she wear a hat or glasses? If so, draw them too! Use different colors to create a picture of your mommy.

A Puppy

Have you ever loved a

little puppy?

If you have

maybe you liked to watch

her sleep

or maybe you liked to feed

him a treat

when she was dirty you may

have washed her soft hair

or even threw a Frisbee or

ball in the air

to watch him run in hopes

he would go fetch

you can have goldfish,

a cat, or a bird

but you may find a puppy

is the best pet

you will have yet

"A Puppy" Questions:

1. Have you ever had a pet? If so, what kind?

2. Have you ever had a puppy of your own? What is his/her name?

3. What kinds of fun things did you or have you done with your puppy?

Ladybugs

See those little

red bugs with polka-dot

spots

and hard shells

they rest then crawl to fly

red bugs, spotted bugs

different bugs, tiny bugs

some are orange too

you can see them

in between blades

of grass

or even under a leaf

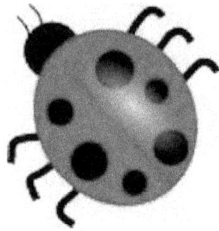

"Ladybugs" Activity

Draw a picture of five ladybugs. Make each one a different color. Use your imagination and give the ladybugs the colors you think they should have!

Down by the Brook

Down by the brook

where the trees and

slithery things meet

I hang out there sometimes

Feeling to cool breeze

Down by the brook

there are colored rocks

and twigs buried deep

in the mud on the side

of the brook

Down by the brook

there is a flowing stream

of sparkling water

moving, catching leaves

and small insects in its flow

Down by the brook

are the mosquitoes

grandma tells me to

watch out for and

even a turtle trudging

along every once in

awhile

Down by the brook

I sit on the edge

where it's cool under

the shade of trees

listening to the birds above

and watching out for more turtles

Down by the brook

you might see a butterfly or two

hovering over a single

flower surrounded by

grass in the mud

of the brook

"Down By the Brook" Activity

Go on a Nature Walk and Record What You Find

The next time you go to the park, or a new place with your family during a vacation, try to explore your surroundings. Find unique rocks, sticks, leaves, flowers, and other items that you can collect. Take a picture of what you see! Be careful not to pick up glass or other dangerous objects. Write a short story about what you did that day and the things you found!

Ten Marbles and a Bag to Put Them In

I found ten marbles

the other day

when Sis' and I

went out to play

Some were tiny

some were large

some had dirt

on them from the garage

Some were red

and some were blue

some were purple like my shoe

We gathered our marbles

with jacks, buttons, pins and rocks

some to hide in my bag

and some to give away

We have ten marbles

and hope to find more

red, blue, purple,

even green and yellow ones

each day

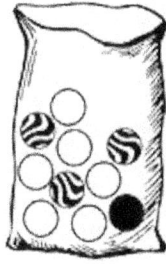

"Ten Marbles" Questions:

1. What is something you like to collect?

2. Have you ever collected baseball or game cards? Rocks? Dolls? Comic books? Describe your collection.

3. Where do you keep your collected items? How many do you have?

4. Take a picture of your collection and paste it here:

Lollipop Swirls

I follow the lollipop swirls

with my eyes

when I unwrap my

big colorful lollipop

I follow the lollipop swirls

with my tongue and I say

'Hmm, hmm, good – this is fun'

I follow the red, white, blue,

yellow, and pink lollipop swirls

they are like dozens of rainbows

meeting in a perfect swirl

My friend asks me

'Well how does it taste?'

I say it tastes plenty sweet like

Strawberry bubblegum

Like mint ice cream

Like brownies

Like apple pie

Like raisin cookies

And chocolate cupcakes

With vanilla icing

I want to savor the taste

I follow the lollipop

swirls as my lollipop

gets smaller and smaller

and smaller

I want another one!

"Lollipop Swirls" Activity

Draw a picture of the lollipop that is described in this poem. Use as many colors as you can and to create a large drawing of the lollipop!

Sleep Tight, Night Light

See the night

fall upon me

Moonlight creep

to come

Come inside my window

tuck me in to sleep

Bright light

moonlight

soft light

night light

Any light

dance around

my room

Come into my window

I will see you soon

Sleep tight

night light

"Sleep Tight, Night Light" Writing Exercise

Write a short poem or story about how you get ready for bed. What time do you go to bed? What do you do before bed? Do you eat a snack? Do you finish your homework? Do you take a bath? Do you talk to your parents or read a book? Do you say your prayers? Be creative! You can even make a rap song about it!

The Boogie Woogie Woogie

I think I hear the sound of footsteps

in my closet

I think I see big white eyes

looking at me,

from behind my chair

Mommie says it's not

what I think it is, she

says, "Baby it's just not there."

She says it's my big

imagination, then

kisses me good night

But when the lights are out

I imagine it

is there watching me

in the night

The Boogie Woogie Woogie

with big eyes, and a big stare

I place my hand over

my eyes and hope

my imagination

takes me

somewhere

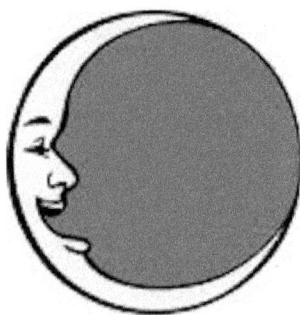

"The Boogie Woogie Woogie" Questions

1. Is there anything that scares you at night?

2. Are you afraid of thunder, lightning, or an imaginary monster?

3. Do you sometimes imagine that there is something creepy in your closet or under your bed? Describe this creepy thing.

Summer Days

I can tell when

summer is coming

Trees lean to catch a

hum against the wind

I hear the bell of an

ice cream truck

My friends and I play hopscotch,

Double dutch, hide and go seek and

Tag - until the street lights come on

I walk with mommy to the

fruit and vegetable market on Saturday

there we buy peaches, cherries, grapes, oranges

and plums

Cornrow braiding mommies braid

their daughters' hair on the porch

The sun sets even later

giving more play time for me

Flowers bloom outside our patio

Smells of barbecue on the grill

Trail across our noses

I have a good day everyday

"Summer Days" Writing Exercise

Write about the most fun experience you had during the summer time? Include who you were with, what you did, where you were, what you saw, and how you felt. You can also include the date, the time of day, and anything else you want to include.

Sky

The sky is turning

blue again

It once was covered

in a gray mask

The sky is turning

blue again

Spring rains visited

the sky's cleansing tears

I wonder when winter

will finally shake hands

with Spring and be shy again

The sky is turning

blue again

Slowly but surely

like molasses running

out of a jar

The sky is turning

blue again and

I welcome it

"Sky" Activity

Draw a picture of the sky in this poem. Use the colors that are mentioned and any other colors you would like.

My Life

My life is a poem

dancing on a page

My life is a leaf floating

down a stream

A kiss of the sun's ray

A butterfly's gentle flutters

A baby's innocent laughter

A river's cleansing waters

A work of beauty and wonder

My life is leaping and jumping

over rainbows

My life is a blessing

"My Life" Writing Exercise

Write a poem about your life. If you had to describe your life, what would it look like? Sound like? Smell like? Taste like? Feel like? What sights and sounds would we hear if we can be in your life? How would we feel if we could feel your life? You can use the poem above, to inspire you to write about your life.

Sky Blues at The Beach

Let me open the

picture book

of my imagination

and tell you

about a sunset celebration

in the sky

Beautiful blues

Like the paint on canvas

Blues that meet the sky

Beach blues so dreamy

I could fly

"Beach Blues" Writing Exercise

What does the sky, ocean and sand look like at your favorite beach. Write about a time when you and your family and friends visited the beach. What did you do there? What did you see? Did you play in the water? Did you build a sand castle?

Whispers of the Wind

Subtle and soft

are the reflections of the sun

Streaming are the waves

of the ocean

Happy to be smiled upon

A whoosh and a whizz

is all that you hear

From the waves

the birds

and the whispers of the wind

"Whispers of the Wind" Questions

1. What does the wind sound like in this poem?

2. What is the wind doing in this poem?

3. What are the waves of the ocean doing?

A Song for Me

Sing me a song

any song

A song that tells,

a song that lulls,

whispers and rocks

me to sleep

Sing me a song

that climbs a willow tree

and rolls down its

drooping branches

like beads of water

off of a slick, slick surface

Sing me a song,

and sing it softly please

Sing me a song

with all of your heart

because every beat

taps with every note

Sing me a song

because with it

I will be pure

rhythm on my own

"A Song for Me" Questions:

1. What is your favorite song?

2. Why type of music do you like to listen to?

3. Do you play a musical instrument? If so, which one?

Puddles, Berries and Rocks

Jump in puddles

get mud on my socks

throw paper planes

walk to collect rocks

Pick the little red berries

see the stain on my shirt

from backyard blackberries

Running in the park

with my sister and my friends

we laugh and shout and tire ourselves out

Go to bed later

and hope to do it

all again

"Puddles, Berries and Rocks" Questions

1. What does the child in this poem jump in?

2. What color are the berries?

3. Who does the child run in the park with?

I Am

I Am
A deep blue marble
With ivory swirls

I Am
A baby's smile
And the twinkle
In a cat's eye

I Am
The run, run, jump
Leap rays of the sun

I Am
The sound of roaring laughter
And the colors of a brilliant rainbow

I Am
A unique me!

"I Am" Writing exercise

Write an "I Am" poem. Write about the things that make you UNIQUE and one of a kind! Write about your favorite colors, favorite activities, and the things that make you happy. You can write your poem in the same form as the one above. Start your poem with the words "I Am."

Use the space below or your own notebook to create your own "I Am" poem.

I Am
By_____(your name)

I Am

_____
_____

I Am

_____
_____

I Am

_____
_____

I Am

_____
_____

I Am

_____
_____

www.ingramcontent.com/pod-product-compliance
Lightning Source LLC
Chambersburg PA
CBHW081638040426
42449CB00014B/3368

* 9 7 8 0 9 7 1 9 0 5 2 4 5 *